Bible Interpretations for the Progressive Christian

John Humble

ISBN: 9781089429081

All Bible quotations in this book are from the King James Version, unless otherwise noted.

DEDICATION

This book is dedicated to all those who dare to question everything they have been taught, and earnestly seek the truth for themselves.

CONTENTS

1 INTRODUCTION: THE SCRIPTURAL CASE AGAINST CHRISTIAN FUNDAMENTALISM

Throughout this book we will explore passages in the Bible, where the Bible is very factually and logically contradicting itself. The purpose of this passage-by-passage analysis is to see if the religious claims of the infallibility and inerrancy of scripture can hold of up logical scrutiny.

Scholars are well aware that many of the Biblical texts come from different Israeli and Jewish communities from different historical periods. Could it be that patriarchal time periods held a different view of who and what God is, when compared the first and second temple period of Judaism?

As we walk through the Bible, we will illustrate and examine how the Bible seems to be presenting, and then in a later historical period, *rewriting* its own theology.

We will begin by showing the amazing contrasts in teaching and doctrine that exist between the two primary sections of the Jewish Bible - the Torah and the Prophets.

The Torah Slammed by Old Testament Prophets

The Competing Faces of Divorce in the Old Testament

Divorce in ancient Israel before the first temple, and also during the 2nd temple period of Jesus, was very one sided in favor of men. In fact, a woman could not legally leave or divorce her husband for any reason - no matter what the husband had done. Men, on the other hand, could decide to divorce their wives at any time for any reason. Women were essentially treated like property, and although under the Torah law both men and women could be equality guilty of committing adultery, in actual practice the woman was blamed for the act. Women simply got a bad deal from ancient Jewish culture and Torah law. It was very similar to the non-existent status that women are given within the context of Islam.

Within the above historical context, a man deciding to divorce his wife essentially meant that her life was over. In most cases, the lady was forced to become a beggar on the street. In others, her family of origin would take her back in. The Biblical reference for this law is in *Deuteronomy* as follows:

Deuteronomy 24:1

When a man hath taken a wife, and married her, and it come to pass that she find no favor in his eyes, **because he hath found some uncleanness in her**: *then let him write her a bill of divorcement, and give it in her hand, and send her out of his house.*

From the beginning, this "uncleanness" was given a very broad range of possible interpretation. It could, in general, refer to *anything* that a husband found to be "wrong" with his wife. In the worst case of it for that cultural and historical community, it could have meant that she was not a virgin when they married. In the best case of "uncleanness", it could be something as simple as having a rude personality. Thus, Old Testament law really stacked the deck against women. Now we will look a section of text from the Old Testament prophets, which will spell out a moral law that seems to be directly opposed to **Deuteronomy 24:1.**

Malachi 2: 13

13 *And this have ye done again, covering the altar of the Lord with tears, with weeping, and with crying out, insomuch that he regardeth not the offering any more, or receiveth it with good will at your hand.*

In this verse, God is having compassion on the women who have been divorced by their husbands. The "tears on the altar" is a reference to these women wailing and crying out to God. One thing that we know about God from many Old Testament stories is that God has special compassion and mercy for classes of people who are oppressed - in this case, divorced women. A few verses later in the same chapter, God makes a much more emphatic statement through the prophet Malachi.

Malachi 2:16

16 *For the Lord, the God of Israel, saith that he hateth putting away: for one covereth violence with his garment, saith the Lord of* *hosts: therefore take heed to your spirit, that ye deal not treacherously.*

Paraphrasing this back to modern English, God is saying that He hates the act of divorce, as it was being committed by men, and He was equating it to committing an act of violence against the woman.

It is most important to realize that this was an evil perpetrated by men in an ancient world where the power of the divorce decision was enjoyed by the man only. In our modern world, where women are equally just as capable of making the decision to divorce, this moral consideration would not apply.

The Competing Faces of Animal Sacrifice in the Old Testament

The laws of the Jews had a lot to do with various animal sacrifices. There are many passage throughout the Torah that mention animal sacrifices, ranging anywhere from turtledoves to bulls. Of course, the small animal sacrifice was included to accommodate the poor. Here is the basic foundational passage.

Exodus 20:24

An altar of earth thou shalt make unto me, and shalt sacrifice thereon thy burnt offerings, and thy peace offerings, thy sheep, and thine oxen: in all places where I record my name I will come unto thee, and I will bless thee.

What is truly amazing about this culture of animal sacrifice, is that while the books of the Torah strongly promote it and support it, the vast majority of other books in Jewish Bible speak out against it.

Given the nature of humans and their religion, it is easy to see why there were second thoughts about "animal sacrifice theology" that began to emerge very quickly. The members of the religion started to treat the ritual of animal sacrifice as a substitute for making any effort to follow the justice, compassion, and mercy towards a fellow human that was prescribed by the Torah.

The book of Psalms is the first book of the Bible to claim that God does not desire animal sacrifices.

> *Sacrifice and offering thou didst not desire. Psalm 40:6*

> *Will I eat of the flesh of bulls, or drink the blood of goats? Psalm 50:13*

> *For thou desirest not sacrifice ... thou delightest not in burnt offerings. Psalm 51:16*

Some of the prophets deliver the same message:

> *I delight not in the blood of bullocks, or of lambs, or of he goats. Isaiah 1:11*

> *Your burnt offerings are not acceptable, nor your sacrifices sweet unto me. Jeremiah 6:20*

> *For I desired mercy, and not sacrifice; and the knowledge of God more than burnt offerings. Hosea 6:6*

> *Shall I come before him with burnt offerings, with calves of a year old?*
> *Will the LORD be pleased with thousands of rams? Micah 6:6-7*

For each of these prophets from the Jewish Bible, if you look at the broader textual context of each verse, you can see that the cry is being made against animal sacrifice because it is being followed while the more important aspects of love and mercy in the Torah are being ignored.

Kosher Food Laws - Man Made?

Jesus and his disciples were living in the 2nd temple period of classic Judaism. During this time, Jews took the Torah scriptures very seriously, much as Jewish people do in our modern times.

Some of the basics of the Torah were well known to even the illiterate in Jewish society. Kosher laws regarding foods that are "clean" or "unclean" were strong examples of Torah code that everyone was familiar with.

The Jews of the second temple period would have considered those laws to be inspired by God, mainly because, fundamentally, the Torah was inspired by God. But was it really, in every single passage of it ? Christian fundamentalists would probably agree with their Jewish counterparts to say a resounding "Yes, the whole Torah was inspired by God". From a Christian point of view, the next passage indicates many possibilities for Kosher law.

Acts 10:11-15

11 And saw heaven opened, and a certain vessel descending upon him, as it had been a great sheet knit at the four corners, and let down to the earth:

12 Wherein were all manner of four footed beasts of the earth, and wild beasts, and creeping things, and fowls of the air.

13 And there came a voice to him, Rise, Peter; kill, and eat.

14 But Peter said, Not so, Lord; for I have never eaten any thing that is common or unclean.

15 And the voice spake unto him again the second time, What God hath cleansed, that call not thou common.

I am sure that this vision threw the Apostle Peter for a roller coaster ride. All of his life, he had been raised in Torah Judaism and had been taught to believe in the Kosher dietary laws. There are two possibilities here:

- God was deciding to change his mind on the Kosher law thing, or
- Human-kind had traditional Hebrew laws on the Kosher diet written to the moral code of the Torah and attributed them to God.

Without drawing any definite conclusions here, we are going to let the reader decide. It seems rather suspicious that Peter is being ask by God now totally disregard what to Peter was inspired holy scripture. Of course, we know that the vision is symbolic of the Gentiles being invited into the family of God. We also see from this passage how God's love is inclusive, whereas humans judge, divide, and separate.

Apostle Paul Writes - "This is just my opinion"

The Apostle Paul is probably our most important New Testament writer by reason of having written 2/3 of it. What may be amazing to Christian Fundamentalist who believe that the epistles were 100% inspired, is that Paul himself, in his own words, did not always think so.

For example, Paul in an epistle writes: "And herein I give my advice" (2 Cor. 8:8-10). Earlier in 1 Corinthians, Paul mentions in chapter 7 that not all of what he is writing is necessarily from the Lord:

1 Cor. 7:10-12

10 And unto the married I command, yet not I, but the Lord, Let not the wife depart from her husband:

11 But and if she depart, let her remain unmarried or be reconciled to her husband: and let not the husband put away his wife.

12 But to the rest speak I, not the Lord: If any brother hath a wife that believeth not, and she be pleased to dwell with him, let him not put her away.

Paul is quite plainly qualifying in this passage that he is giving his human opinion and the Holy Spirit is not necessarily speaking through him.

Thus, Paul actually admits in his letters that he is not always writing from Divine Inspiration.

Further to this point, Paul admits that he desires to seek the approval of the apostles leading the church of Jerusalem for the version of the gospel that he is teaching. From *Galatians 2:2* we have

> **2** *And I went up by revelation, and communicated unto them that gospel which I preach among the Gentiles, but privately to them which were of reputation, lest by any means I should run, or had run, in vain.*

Further reading into chapter 2 of *Galatians* gives us the broader context. Paul is seeking a private meeting with Peter, James, and John - men who are widely recognized as the leaders of the Jerusalem church. The purpose of that meeting is to have them privately review the version of the gospel message that he has been preaching. In Acts chapter 15, the Jerusalem church leadership approves of his message, but with certain stipulations.

If Paul had been 100% certain of his own divine inspiration, there would have been no reason to seek review and approval from the Jerusalem apostles.

The Woman with the Menstrual Disorder

The woman with the issue of blood is a well-known story that appears in three of the gospel narratives - *Matthew 9:20–22, Mark 5:25–34*, and *Luke 8:43–48*. The language in the KJV "issue of blood" is simply an old fashion way of referring to a menstrual disorder. This poor lady had no monthly relief whatsoever from menstruation. To make matters worse for her, any person who touches her is ceremonially unclean according to *Leviticus 15:19*.

The condition of being ceremonially unclean was not necessarily the end of the world in ancient temple Judaism, but it was extremely inconvenient. A man could not visit the temple until the next day, and if he mistakenly had intercourse with his wife during her menstrual period, he would be barred from the temple for seven days.

Most leadership figures in the Jewish religion of the time period were quite snobbish about trying to stay ceremonially clean all the time according to this law in Leviticus.

All of the above is to explain why this woman would fall to the ground in fear after reaching out and touching Jesus. *It is important to keep in mind that the whole of Leviticus is at this time being regarded as the inspired word of God.* From a legalistic point of view, Jesus became *ceremonially unclean* at the very moment that the woman with the menstrual disorder touched him.

Of course, much to the lady's surprise, Jesus is not the least bit concerned about the fact that he has just become ceremonially unclean. He openly hails and admires the faith that this lady has had.

The reaction of Jesus is a perfect example of <u>love being superior to legalism</u>. Did Jesus even recognize the divine inspiration of *Leviticus 15:19*? Given that all conservative fundamentalist Jews of his generation would have taken *Leviticus 15:19* very seriously, it is interesting that Jesus does not even appear to acknowledge the existence of this law in his behavior towards this woman.

When Jesus Discusses Divorce with Pharisees

Now, let us take a look at that whopper New Testament passage (*Matthew 19*) where Jesus completely disregards the divine inspiration of the *Deuteronomy 24* :

> *7 They say unto him, Why did Moses then command to give a writing of divorcement, and to put her away?*
>
> *8 He saith unto them, <u>Moses because of the hardness of your hearts suffered you to put away your wives: but from the beginning it was not so</u>.*
>
> *9 <u>And I say unto you</u>, Whosoever shall put away his wife, except it be for fornication, and shall marry another, committeth adultery: and whoso marrieth her which is put away doth commit adultery.*

During the life of Jesus, the Torah, the first 5 books of Moses in our Bible, were considered by most of the Jews to be the inspired Word of the living God. There was also a widespread Jewish believe in the **infallibility** and in the ***inerrancy of scripture.***

The Old Testament Torah scripture on putting away one's wife was the scripture being discussed. By saying "Moses because of the hardness of your hearts suffered you", Jesus is essentially saying that Moses wrote that in because <u>you as a people culturally demanded it</u>. THIS IS IN TOTAL OPPOSITION TO A JEWISH FUNDAMENTALIST BELIEF THAT THE TORAH SCRIPTURE ON DIVORCE WAS INSPIRED BY GOD!! **Thus, in the *logical* consideration of this New Testament passage it is impossible to say that Jesus was a fundamentalist or that he believed in the inerrancy of His own scripture (the Torah).**

For Christian Fundamentalists who believe in a certain rigid method of interpreting the Bible, **a logical person coming from a totally different world religion would have just cause to wonder and ask** what the higher priority is for a Christian fundamentalist?

Is it -

- being adamant about 100% of all scripture being Divinely inspired and therefore completely inerrant?, or
- following <u>the example of Jesus Christ, the Son of God,</u> in how He treated scripture in a more balanced and less absolute way?

If the previous paragraphs were speaking of any person, other than Jesus, most readers would conclude that the person responding to the Pharisees is either a Jewish "Liberal" or "a Progressive". Relative to His religious peers in the first century, Jesus was most certainly a Progressive.

The motivation for legalism and rigidity is fear. We are not talking about the "fear of the Lord" mentioned in the Bible which is a different kind of fear altogether. The fear we are talking about is sourced from a combination our guilty sin consciousness, and the belief that God is just in the most harsh way, without mercy.

This fear and belief in a non-merciful Creator has caused both Jewish and Christian theology to evolve and develop the belief in an everlasting punishment. Thus, the subject of Hell is the content of our next chapter.

2 THE BIBLICAL EVIDENCE FOR THE NON-EXISTENCE OF HELL

Ever since I was a small child, I have had questions about what the religion of my upbringing was trying to teach me. The question of the fairness of Hell has always been one of those questions. Even in our human created legal system in the United States, we have a general principle in our judicial system of "let the punishment fit the crime". We are also taught that although God is JUST and FAIR, and that a person who makes mistakes, hurts a few people, and maybe even has some bad habits for 70 to 80 years of human life must spend ETERNITY in Hell. Even as a small child I did not understand how an eternity of torture, pain, and punishment was a fair consequence for evil acts occurring over a very limited mortal life span. As we take a journey through many verses in the Bible from beginning to end, we will see that our Creator is indeed a JUST God, and that Hell does not necessary mean what the leaders of our religion have tried to convey.

We will learn some things from the scriptures about Divine consequences that will exist, and we will see what kind of places or states of being were really being conveyed by the word "Hell" in the way that the New Testament uses the word.

The belief in Hell, or some version of it on the part of most world religions, stems from a natural human need to believe that the Creator is **fair** and **just**. Thus, in a circumstantial world where cruel, unkind, and unjust people seem to get ahead in life, our need for justice demands that on some scheme of reality beyond what we perceive with our five physical senses, there must be a principle of justice or reciprocity in the Universe.

In looking at the doctrine of Hell, we need to ask ourselves if the Jewish audience that was contemporary with the life of Christ and His apostles also believed in an existence of Hell. After all, if the Messiah is coming to save the Jews, *what exactly is He saving the Jews from?* Thus, in order to support that Hell exists in exactly the way that our Christian theology describes it, it follows logically, that it must have existed that way in the minds of first century Jews. Therefore, in our review and study of all the scriptures containing words that were translated "Hell", we are going to dive deeper into a Jewish cultural and historical explanation of what these words meant to the first century Jewish mind.

The word "Hell" as it appears in the King James Version of the New Testament is sourced from 2 commonly occurring words – the Greek place name Hades and the Hebrew place name GeHenna. In all places where "Hell" is mentioned in the New Testament, it is these translated words behind the scenes. In the following sections of this chapter, we will give a historical background on each of these places. Some writers on this topic will say that Sheol is a third word, but as we will see later, this is actually a synonym for Hades. In this chapter we will look at some of these key words that were translated "Hell" in our Bible, and the impact that culture and translation has had upon how we perceive their meaning.

The Words, Their History, and Basic Meaning

A History of "Hades"

This is the underworld of pagan Greek mythology. It was the natural home of certain Greek gods, and it was the place where the souls of the dead were kept. There was a level of final justice to be distributed in the Greek underworld. A good man would live forever in the peaceful region of Hades known as the Elysian Fields. An uncompromisingly cruel and evil man would go do a very deep abyss section of Hades that was called Tartarus.

In its earliest developments, the Hades underworld contained no distinction of different places that good or evil people would go to, and Tartarus was a place meant only as a prison for Greek gods who had fallen out of favor with their leadership. The separation of Hades into a heaven-like or Hell-like division is a development occurring much later.

Hades is relevant to the Biblical discussion, because as a word, it appears approximately 10 or 11 times in the original Greek New Testament, and in English it is always translated "Hell".

The version of the Old Testament scriptures that was most widely read in the first century was the Septuagint. This version was a translation of the Torah and the Prophets from Hebrew into Greek. The afterlife underworld that is specifically mentioned in the Hebrew Scriptures is Sheol. Thus, throughout the Septuagint version, you will find the word "Hades" where "Sheol" had been in the Hebrew version.

According to the 9th chapter of Ecclesiastes, the souls of the dead in Sheol are hardly fitting what we would call a human existence - without thought, emotion, wisdom, etc. There are also many references within Job and the Psalms of Sheol having no light or sound – a place of complete sensory deprivation. The Greek Hades, by comparison, is a much more colorful afterlife existence – even in its "punishment" section.

This original Hebrew concept of Sheol does not really change that much until the 12th chapter of Daniel, where the concept of the resurrection is first introduced. From that point on in the development of Jewish theology, Sheol is a temporary holding place for the dead until the day of resurrection.

By the time of Jesus, the concept of Sheol has become greatly Hellenized, and made to look like a Jewish version of the complex Hades realm with all of its divisions.

A History of "Gehenna"

This word is a Greek form of the name Hinnom, who was a character in the Old Testament that had a valley named after him. Thus, the "the valley of Hinnom" is what the word Gehenna literally refers to. With Jerusalem on top of Mount Zion, this valley stretched around the south to southwest edge of the city.

In the minds of first century Jews, Gehenna had become a place of extreme defilement and uncleanness, and it was associated with the historical guilt and shame of Israel with respect to idol worship. The Israelites had used this valley at one time to sacrifice their own children to a demonic entity known as Moloch.

For most of its history after King Josiah ended the idolatrous practices there, it was used by the inhabitants of Jerusalem as a place to dump and burn garbage, and the bodies of executed murderers were dumped there as well. By the time of Christ it was also being used as a place to dump sewage from the city. In order to keep the maggot-invested garbage and sewage from growing too much, several fires were kept constantly burning.

There is a direct reference to Gehenna as a place of divine judgment in *Isaiah* 66:24:

> *And they shall go forth, and look upon the carcasses of the men that have transgressed against me: for their worm (the maggots) shall not die, neither shall their fire be quenched; and they shall be an abhorring unto all flesh.*

In the broader context of Isaiah 66 this is talking about the Messianic Age, which corresponds to the 1000 years of peace under the leadership of Christ mentioned in Revelation. Every time you see the phrase "their worm dieth not" in the KJV version of the New Testament, it is a reference to this prophecy in Isaiah.

This is, of course, a picture of bodies that have been disposed of as garbage after a battle has ended. The Old Testament prophets repeatedly warned that Israel would be defeated by their enemies if they did not repent and walk uprightly before the Lord.

Failure to repent of rebellion against their God would result in the bodies of Israeli soldiers being thrown on to Gehenna's flames and being eaten by maggots (worms). This is the Divine Judgment consequence of being thrown away as garbage just before the 1000 year Messianic Age begins.

Thus, we see from this study that the word Gehenna, that word most often translated "Hell", did not really refer to an *everlasting afterlife* punishment in its original context, although it was most certainly referring to a consequence of unbelief and disobedience.

First Century Afterlife Beliefs: A House Divided

There were two different audiences of Judaism that Jesus and the apostles had to deal with.

Before discussing the differences between afterlife belief systems of the 2nd Temple Period Jews (the era of Judaism that Jesus and his disciples came from), it is important to devote at least a few paragraphs to the common original thread of afterlife belief that both the Sadducees and the Pharisees evolve from.

Afterlife Beliefs - The Ancient Israeli Period

Has anybody ever wondered why it was such a big deal to promise Abraham that his descendants would be as many as the stars of heaven? Wouldn't he want something more than that? The answer is that he would have wanted much more - immortality perhaps - if he had the ability to believe that he could have had this. In the mind of his generation, the grave was the end, and the next best alternative was to have many descendants, and to be remembered as a great name amongst all of those descendents for many generations. Thus, God was promising Abraham the closest thing to eternal life, that Abraham could accept or believe in. Of course, the Great I AM was also satisfying an agenda of redeeming and reclaiming back all nations from the dominion of other fallen celestial beings, but that is a subject beyond the scope of this book.

In the previous discussion where we talked about Sheol, we mentioned that Sheol was just "the grave", and considered to be a state of complete nothingness and a memorial for the living only, until the book of Daniel. Only with that book, does Sheol get promoted to the position of being a holding place for people until the day of judgment, and a mode of human sensory existence beyond the physical body. Even many generations after the writing of Daniel, the holding place was interpreted to be an area where the human soul was essentially asleep until judgment day, regardless of whether or not the individual had lived a righteous life.

Hellenized beliefs about Sheol's similarity to Hades do not start to enter a few Jewish sectarian groups until some of the non-Biblical Jewish literature starts to get written during the Greek empire period. This paragraph marks the spot where Sadducee and Pharisee afterlife beliefs start to split into diverging paths.

The Sadducees

On one side, you had the Sadducees, who rejected the book of *Daniel,* and who did not believe in any form of conscious existence after death. Remember when Jesus stood before the High Priest Caiaphas and identified himself as the Son of Man coming in the clouds (*Daniel,* Chapter 7)? The response of the High Priest was to get so offended that he tore his robe. In the belief system of the Jerusalem priests, as a Sadducee, the very notion of a Divine Son of Man or anything out of the book of *Daniel* was blasphemy. For the Sadducee student, there was no such thing as the resurrection, and Sheol meant nothing more than the grave. A Sadducee would completely reject the Hellenized view of Sheol that resembled Hades.

Lastly, in the Sadducee mind, being thrown into burning Gehenna garbage dump was the physical punishment from God associated with Israel being defeated in war, with no afterlife implications whatsoever.

Thus, even in their non-spiritual world view, Jesus was also reaching the Sadducee with prophetic warnings to repent, and reminding them of the Gehenna consequence possibility - a consequence that did eventually reach them in 70 A.D. when General Titus destroys Jerusalem.

The Pharisees

Then, on the other extreme, you have the Pharisees who were the spiritualists of Judaism for their generation. This group believed that the book of *Daniel* was God's inspired word, and that the resurrection mentioned within it was as real as the air they breathed. The Pharisee also believed in a Hellenized concept of Sheol where people were alive and fully conscious of whatever afterlife consequences they were experiencing - a belief very similar to the Greek myth of Hades (in contrast to the mindless, emotionless existence of Sheol depicted in *Ecclesiastes* and the *Psalms*).

The view of Gehenna for the Pharisees was similar to the Sadducee belief on the Divine Judgment of being defeated in war, but there is also a popular historical speculation that they also probably used it as a symbol for an afterlife Divine consequence. The picture of Hades and Abraham's Bosom that appears in the rabbinic parable given by Jesus also appears in Midrash and Talmudic literature of the Jews some 400 to 500 years later when the Talmudic works were being compiled. Although it was not written down until 400 to 500 years later in the Talmud, the fact that it was eventually written gives rise to a probable speculation that this parable was at least a part of some Pharisee rabbinical oral tradition during the lifetime of Jesus.

Within the Jewish faith the house is divided even now in modern times on the subject of the afterlife.

The Hasidim and many other Orthodox groups that follow the Jewish Kabballah hold to a belief in reincarnation. For them, the concept of "resurrection" in the book of Daniel is actually a metaphor for "reincarnation". For them, Gehenna represents a horrible life that someone was incarnated into, as punishment for sins committed in a previous life. According to the Hasidim, for the righteous, there is an incarnation to occur within the end-times "heaven on earth" peaceful Age of the Messiah, and the wicked will not incarnate during this period at all.

There are also many Orthodox Jewish groups that adhere to a belief in Paradise Eden as a region of Sheol, and a Gehenna as a lower region of Sheol. The Paradise Eden is similar to the garden of God in the book of Genesis, but much more glorified and peaceful with God's Presence, according to the Orthodox Jews.

With the Orthodox Jewish Gehenna, even for the most evil and cruel people, the place is NOT eternal. After 12 months, according to Talmudic references, you either get promoted to Paradise Eden or you cease to exist (and the ceasing to exist applies only to those who were at that "Adolph Hitler" level of evil).

The preceding paragraphs should make it plane to the reader that the Jewish religion has been, and probably will always be divided on the subject of the afterlife. Thus, it should be understood in appropriate context that it was a specific Jewish audience that Jesus was trying to reach with his "Rich Man and Lazarus Parable" parable. If you examine the context of the gospel of *Luke,* you can see that he was directly addressing the Pharisees when he was presenting this parable. This was a parable, which, according to Talmud records, had been widely known in rabbinical circles. Had he been talking to a group of Sadducee Jews, the plot and setting elements of his story would have been completely different. The author's conclusion is that the use Jesus made of the Hades version of Sheol was for the purpose of reaching his Pharisee audience. It was not necessarily an endorsement of that particular afterlife belief as being the real thing.

The Rich Man and Lazarus Parable

There have always been very different schools of thought on how to interpret this parable. Some have said that it is a literal prophetic account of a real person's actual afterlife experience. On the other extreme, some have called it a parable of Christ with a purely symbolic meaning.

The literary context of this in Luke's gospel would indicate that it is a parable, following immediately after a long string of other parables told back-to-back, and all directed at the Pharisees, who were face-to-face with Jesus, and listening to Jesus.

The author would like to assert that neither of these considerations are important. Jesus was clearly trying to reach his audience - the Pharisees in this case. His only hope in getting through to them would be to break down their self-delusion that they were in right standing with God, just on account of being children of Abraham who knew the Torah better than most people.

In the verses leading up to the parable, Jesus teaches the Pharisees with other parables and sayings. He challenges them to rise to higher moral standards of love, mercy, and justice than merely what the Torah states. Knowing that they are the sect that believes in a spiritual afterlife, he then proceeds to hit them right where they live.

Whether or not Jesus held to and believed in the same afterlife dogma of the Pharisees was not important. What was most important to our Lord and Savior is that through his speech he could somehow inspire them to repentance.

It was not the story itself that came to us through Divine Inspiration, but rather it was the use and adaptation of the story by Jesus Christ that came by the inspiration of the Holy Spirit. According to Thomas B. Thayer, in his classic *The Origin & History of the Doctrine of Endless Punishment*, the story of the Rich Man and Lazarus had already been used by many other rabbinical teachers and was originally a parable sourced from a Jewish work called Gemara Babylonicum. Jesus, in true rabbinical teaching style, adapted this story in his address to the Pharisees.

The Pharisees had not been treating the poor, the fatherless, and the widow with the justice and mercy that the Torah prescribes. The Pharisees had resources and an esteemed level of education, yet they did not use their position nor their resources in acts of kindness and justice to the poor.

By throwing this particular afterlife parable at the Pharisees, Jesus is trying to warn them that their opportunity to perform acts of charity and mercy is NOW, and that in a next form of existence they may no longer be in the favored position relative to the Gentiles, if they squander their current opportunity to perform acts of righteousness and mercy.

The other criticism that Jesus is casting upon the Pharisee is their failure to be the light in the world that they should be. The Pharisee was aligned with synagogue houses of worship, which means that this sect would have been sprinkled amongst the nations.

The name "Lazarus" is a Greek form of "Eliezer" - the name of Abraham's Gentile servant. Abraham once thought that Eliezer would be his only heir before God made a special promise. Thus, at a deeper level of meaning, this parable is also a way of warning the Pharisees that the believing Gentiles could soon replace them in Abraham's family if they did not repent.

Thus, we must conclude that, in the scriptural context of His address to the Pharisees, this parable actually had very little to do with the need to establish an afterlife doctrine.

A New Testament Analysis of Afterlife Words - Tracing the Word "Hell" through the New Testament

As a recap of what we covered earlier in the book, the appearance of "Hell" in the KJV comes from 3 Greek words - Hades, Tartarus, and a Greek form of the Hebrew place-name GeHenna.

We can exclude Tartarus from consideration, because it is exclusively reserved as a prison for fallen angels - essentially nonhuman entities.

We have covered that Hades basically comes to us because of it being the Greek translation of the Hebrew Sheol in the Septuagint, which was the Greek translation of the Old Testament of that time period. We also mentioned that Hellenized afterlife beliefs related to the Greek myth of Hades had greatly influenced the Jewish concept of *Sheol*, which was only a reference to "the grave" in its original Old Testament context.

Another historical commentary on this foreign Greek influence can be seen in other Semitic groups. From the religion of Islam, Quran contains 77 references to GeHenna, but no references whatsoever to Hades. It is quite conceivable that even in the first century, Jews were much more metropolitan, modernistic, and Greek cultured than many of their Arabic and other Semitic counterparts. This may be the background reason as to why the Greek Hades afterlife place does not even register on the radar for Islam.

The New Testament refers to Hades as a place distinct from GeHenna. Unlike GeHenna, Hades typically conveys neither fire nor punishment but forgetfulness. (https://en.wikipedia.org/wiki/Gehenna) [The reader will recall the fact that the Rich Man has an unknown forgotten name in Christ's parable that utilizes the *Hades* concept.]

The use of GeHenna as a place of consequence is mentioned as "Topheth" a few times in the Old Testament. In *Isaiah* 30:30 it is designated as the place where the bodies of the soldiers of the Assyrian army will be burned. Then later in *Isaiah* 66:24 it is noted as a place where the bodies of the enemies of the Messiah will be burned, near the beginning of the Messianic Age of peace.

There are 12 occurrences of GeHenna in the New Testament. Of great significance is the fact that 11 of them are statements made by Jesus recorded in the four Gospels, with 7 of those being in *Matthew*. <u>Thus, in the formation of any doctrine or interpretation around GeHenna, understanding the audience and the historical context for *Matthew* is important.</u>

With *Isaiah* being the Old Testament work that is most rich in Davidic Messianic prophecies, and in consideration of the fact that *Matthew* was written for a Jewish audience, the verses from *Isaiah* about GeHenna that we just mentioned in the last few paragraphs are extremely important for understanding the context which Jesus is talking from when he uses the word in *Matthew*.

The *GeHenna* consequence being mentioned in *Isaiah* relates to either being against the Messiah or simply being rebellious against God.

There are other New Testament references, where the word GeHenna is not being used in the Greek, but the reader can tell from the context that

GeHenna is what is being referred to. Examples of this would be *Matthew* 13:42 and 2 *Thessalonians* 1:8.

Was this punitive consequence, according to scripture, <u>meant to be forever?</u> To explore this question, we will look at the Greek words behind English translations into words such as "eternal" and "everlasting".

A New Testament Analysis of Afterlife Words - Tracing the Words "Eternal" and "Everlasting" through the New Testament

Every time we see the word "eternal" in the New Testament King James version, the Greek word behind it is either "*aion*" or "*aionios*". Aionios is "*aion*" + "*ios*" - and adjective form of the Greek noun. *Aion* means age, and it is the direct equivalent of our English word *eon*. The suffix *-ios* means pertaining to or relating to. So, aion-ios properly means "pertaining to the eon" or more simply "relating to an age or its duration."

This is extremely significant because this direct translation conveys that there are actually fewer references to a concepts of "eternity" and "everlasting" within the Bible than most readers of the King James version would be led to believe. This has a huge impact on the actual meaning of several key verses. For example, we could have more accurately translated *John* 3:16

> *For God so loved the world, that he gave his only begotten Son, that whosoever believeth in him should not perish, but have [aionios zoe].*

There is a more appropriate translation than the "everlasting life" given in the KJV, such as "age enduring life" or "the eon of life", where the latter phrase is probably the closest match when one considers the context of the 1000 year period of peace on earth - the Messianic Age - which "the eon of life" would have been a common expression for.

<u>The promise of being rewarded as one of the ruling righteous during the Messianic Age was the actual "heaven" or "eon of life" that most of the Jews of the first century were looking for.</u> What they longed for and yearned for was for Israel to have its national sovereignty back with the Messiah on the throne.

Depending on one's standing with God, the individual would either become a joint-heir and joint-ruling relationship with the Messiah over the entire world during this age under the conditions of *Isaiah* chapter 9, or the individual would be subject to suffering and social marginalization during this period.

As Christians, we understand the "eon of life" from *John* 3:16 to mean a spiritually abundant experience of life, and yes, one that will last for ***eternity***, but that word is a characteristic of our modern day religious belief alone, and its modern day meaning is not supported by the historical cultural context of the verse, nor its use of Greek.

The same Greek term "aionios" is also used in passages that talk about fire and judgment, which, according to the actual meaning of this word ARE NOT ETERNAL in the sense that we throw this word around in modern day religious terminology. The meaning of "for the eon" or "enduring to the end of the age" would be the same, and in the broader context it would refer to the punitive fate of the non-believer during the 1000 year period.

There are a total of 71 occurrences of "aionios" in the New Testament, and out of those, only 4 of them are used in the context of Divine Punishment. (Matthew 18:8, Matthew 25:41, Matthew 25:46, Mark 3:29). In each of them, "to the end of the age" or the "duration of the eon" is still the most correct translation of this term.

There is a scene described in *Isaiah* 66:24 where the final battle between the Lord and His enemies has taken place, and the bodies of the evil army are being burned in GeHenna on the garbage heap. This chapter also talks about the beginning of the Age of the Messiah on earth after this war.

There is a strong parallel between this chapter in Isaiah and what appears in *Revelation* 19:19 of the KJV:

> ***19*** *And I saw the beast, and the kings of the earth, and their armies, gathered together to make war against him that sat on the horse, and against his army.*

The passage concludes with the Beast and his army leaders being cast into the lake of fire, with the remnant of the armies being slain by the sword proceeding out of the mouth of Christ.

What is very interesting about this verse in Revelation is that **it leaves behind as survivors all of the followers of the Beast who were not marching in this war, by reason of being non-military civilians.**

The idea of Divine Justice here (within the first century Jewish cultural mind) is that the ruling and dominating class in the world will no longer be the non-believing sinners. No longer will the politicians and governors be corrupt and dishonest people. **<u>In this world, only a just, meek, God-fearing person will advance to power and leadership.</u>** Those who have been non-believers and/or followers of the Beast will be *lower class citizens in this world*, and will be extremely marginalized during this 1000 year period. They will now be subjugated and ruled by the just and righteous followers of the Jewish Messiah, and the world will be under the rule of the Godly for this particular <u>eon of time</u>. It is in this way that "aionios" fire, or "aionios" damnation, or "aionios" punishment, most certainly lasts a long time – to the end of an entire eon or age, but it is not "eternal" according to the way that our modern day English religion treats the word. Thus, the word "eternal" is a mistranslation that has been historically embraced for quite some time. Of course, even during this period or eon of 1000 years, those who did not become followers of the beast have an opportunity to repent towards believing and obeying the Gospel of Christ, and join the ruling class.

Another form of the word, "aidios", was only used two places in the New Testament. It is translated "everlasting" in the KJV. In the epistle of Jude, it does appear as a punitive reference to the story from the book of *Enoch*, where fallen angels were forcefully bound so that they could not come into contact with the human race. We know from the book of *Revelation* chapter 9 that these beings were later released in order bring plagues upon the empire of the Beast. Thus, the use of "aidios" cannot be referring to "everlasting" in a *literal* sense. We know that the locust-like demons are the very same fallen angels from the book of *Enoch* because *Enoch* **is the only piece of literature placed within 2nd temple period** Judaism where the concept of the Abyss is mentioned as a prison for non-human evil entities.

There are many authors on this topic that have gone so far as to say that the concept of eternity came to the early Church Fathers through Neoplatonism schools of philosophy, and does not appear in the New

Testament at all.

While Augustine and many other notable Church Fathers were certainly influenced by Plato – as admitted by them in their own writings – that hypothesis on the lack of a New Testament "eternity" concept is not entirely correct. For example, where Revelation 11:15 of the KJV says

...and He shall reign forever and ever

that last phrase, "forever and ever" comes from two forms of **aion** that are joined together - **aionas ton aionon** - which literally means "the eons of the eons", or, in other words, what we think of when we say "eternity". Thus, it is incorrect to say that the New Testament is blind to the concept of eternity. Often times when two forms of the Greek word "aion" are joined together in the same phrase, our modern concept of "eternity" is exactly what is being meant.

The point to bring out in this chapter is that most of the uses of "eternity", "eternal", or "everlasting" with respect to life or punishment being mentioned in a New Testament verse do not literally mean "forever without end", but refers to an eon - a very long period of time. In the context of *Isaiah* and other Messianic prophecies in the Hebrew scriptures, this eon of time is 1000 years - the Messianic Age.

With this chapter, we have seen how the real source of the Hell doctrine is probably GeHenna, given the fact that GeHenna and Hades are completely different places, with one of them being merely a transformed version of the Hebrew Sheol – "the grave".

We have also seen from the Isaiah context that GeHenna is the specific Divine Consequence of being defeated in war and having the bodies of your soldiers dumped on the burning garbage heap that was in the valley of GeHenna.

Finally, after looking at the Greek words behind those NT translations of "everlasting" and "eternal", we see that the punishment or consequence from God is not necessarily meant to last forever and be without end.

The Historical Development of Christian Afterlife Doctrine

Augustine was the first to write down a formal theology on the doctrine of Hell. In his work, *City of God*, he addresses the objections made by church leaders before him on the concept of eternal pain and suffering. Augustine was in agreement with those early theologians who asserted the teaching of eternal torment for the lost. We will see in the following paragraphs where those early theologians got their ideas from.

A few generations after the apostles of Christ, Athenagoras (A.D. 133–190) emerged as a scholar and Christian convert in Alexandria, Egypt. He was a devoted student of Greek philosophy before his conversion, after which he became a famous theologian. Athenagoras was **the very first within church history to publish a written teaching on the immortality of the human soul**, for both righteous and wicked people. He concludes in his theology that the suffering of punishment on the part of the wicked is also eternal after the death of the body.

In the last chapter, <u>we provided evidence to show that a concept of eternity is never used with the New Testament within the context of an afterlife consequence.</u> Thus, we must conclude that Athenagoras did not get his source information on the eternal nature of the soul from the Greek New Testament scriptures. Where did he get it from then? From Britannica's reference, "Athenagoras' theology "is strongly tinged with Platonism" (*Encyclopedia Britannica*, s.v. "Athenagoras," 11th ed., 831). The philosophy of Plato as actually used by many early theologians in the formation of church doctrine. According to church historian Dr. L.E. Froom,

> *"It is to be particularly noted that all Christian Fathers who use this 'immortal soul' phrase or thought were not only familiar with but likewise in accord with this position in the writing of Plato. And it is also to be observed that* **none of such early Christian writers ever sought for support for this doctrine by primary appeal to Scripture,** *but had recourse instead to arguments similar to those used by Plato" (Dr. LeRoy E. Froom, Conditionalist Faith of Our Fathers*
>
> *[1965], vol. 1, p. 954).*

Alternative Biblical Views on Afterlife Consequence

While the eternal punishment is not necessarily supported by the original Greek New Testament, the consequence of divine consequence most certainly is. The eastern teaching known as Karma, or the law of the effect, appears in our Bible under *Galations* 6:7:

> *"Be not deceived; God is not mocked: for whatsoever a man soweth, that shall he also reap."*

What this means is that energy, thought, action on the part of an individual will always eventually result in that same individual being on the ***receiving end*** of that same energy, thought, and action.

The receiving end is not something that would be eternal or everlasting, because the seeds were not being sown over an everlasting time period either.

There have been near death experience reports on the part of a certain people (and many autobiographical books have been published on this) who report that while they are watching what appears to be a video replay of their entire earthly life, the tape slows down on those events where they are causing harm to a fellow human, and for a few moments, they are in the shoes of their victims, experiencing whatever pain , anguish, or fear that the victim experienced. After finishing the video tape of their life, the experience is over, and new afterlife experiences can begin.

The near death accounts such as the above, sound really far-fetched to a scientific mind, but when you put their experiences in the context of the Biblical principle of sowing and reaping, it makes perfect sense.

It also makes sense, that given that the person is not harming others forever and throughout all eternity, the consequences also would not last forever.

Here is a thought provoking question. What if, even in an afterlife context, a person **refuses to repent** of evil and goes on trying to hurt, disrespect, or mistreat others encountered in the afterlife experience? The answer is that Galatians 6:7 expresses a cosmic principle that is always in effect, regardless of whether or not the actor has a physical body. Thus, a person could theoretically experience something similar to "everlasting Hell" in an afterlife experience if that person is still continuously attempting to create that experience for others, and not repenting of that activity.

In the next two chapters we are going to deal with the issues regarding the treatment of women and homosexuals, and we are going to focus on many scriptures that have been used to support common social beliefs and agendas.

3 WERE JESUS AND PAUL GENDER EQUALITY ACTIVISTS?

For most of my life, I have been subject to comments about women while listening to a sermon. Most of those comments were stating men to be superior and women to be like children. Being a typical male, for many years growing up, I did not think much about this preaching, and I must admit that for a brief period of my youth, I actually believed it. After all, the preacher was quoting scripture from the Bible, the inspired word of God. As a young Christian fundamentalist, it was impossible for me to find fault with any message that seemed to be coming right from the pages of the Bible.

What I did not realize at the time, is that it is very easy to take scriptures from the Bible out of context, for the purpose of supporting *any agenda or desired propaganda.* I don't blame the preachers for this. They were genuinely believing their interpretation of the verses that they were reading, and thus, their act of twisting certain scripture verses out of context was totally unconscious on their part.

In this book, we are going analyze the scriptures about women that are commonly quoted, and we are going to get at the original intended meaning. This original intended meaning can only found by having full knowledge of the historical time period, the culture of the audience, and the specific situation or common belief that is being addressed by the passage. In other words, we are going to do much more research homework around specific passage of scripture than most pulpit pastors are willing to do. The return on our investment for making this greater contextual research effort is that we will arrive at what was, most likely, the originally intended meaning of the passage.

Near the end of the Gospel of John, there is a passage that says that if all the works and deeds of Jesus were to be recorded, there would not be enough books in the world to contain all of that information. A hidden clue from St. John is that fact that the leaders of the first century church are picking which stories and sayings from Jesus that the audience is going to hear.

Thus, when we start to see the examples of how Jesus treats women in the gospels, we are, in fact, seeing a view of women that the original Apostolic

Fathers of the church wanted us to see. As we are about to see in the next chapter, the first generation team of Apostles were way ahead of their time on the social issue of gender equality.

How Jesus Treated Women

The first example is the woman with the issue of blood. This story appear in the 9th chapter of *Matthew* and in other gospels.

The text describes this lady as having had an "issue of blood" for twelve years and also having spent a small fortune on doctor's fees. She said to herself over and over again, "if I but touch the hem of his garment, I shall be made whole." The term "issue of blood" is synonymous with a menstrual disorder.

The old Torah law dictates that no one is allowed to come into contact with a woman that is in the middle of her menstrual cycle. The consequence is being declared unclean until the morning of the next day, and no one was allowed to come into physical contact with a person who had become unclean during this period. This also meant that you were not allowed within the Temple until the morning of the next day.

This is a very short period of time to be unclean, and yet pious pride caused many rabbis and Pharisees to shun women in public on the pretense of being more holy. Thus, it was very easy to understand why this woman fell to her knees in fear (chapter 5 in *Mark*), as if she had done something horrible by touching Him.

How did Jesus reach to a menstruating woman touching him? Well, if you read the passage, you find that He was so impressed by the woman's faith that his being made temporarily "unclean" was not at all a concern. He had great compassing on the lady, and he treated her with great respect.

The next story comes out of *Matthew* 15:22.

> *And, behold, a woman of Canaan came out of the same coasts, and cried unto him, saying, Have mercy on me, O Lord, thou Son of David; my daughter is grievously vexed with a devil.*

For a few dialog exchanges, Jesus refused to help this woman at first, but he was not basing on her being a woman, but on the fact that she was a non-Jew. She had an uncompromising faith in the LOVE of the one true God, and she believed that this man Jesus was God's representative on earth. Thus, when she said

> *And she said, Truth, Lord: yet the dogs eat of the crumbs which fall from their masters' table.*

Jesus could take no more dialog after this. Her faith had completely one Him over. "O, woman, great is thy faith", He said.

In this story Jesus actually had two good reasons to ignore a request: 1) a woman is making the request, and 2) she is a Canaanite.

What do these passages say about the way God responds to faith? Based on these stories, could there be any gender bias where faith is concerned ? The answer is obvious.

There are different versions of a woman walking into a house to anoint Jesus with oil or ointment. Anointing the head of an honored guest was a typical custom of the time period Thus, it is not outside the realm of possibility that, where two different gospels tell slightly different versions, they could actually be referring to separate events. In each example, the men in the room were very critical of the woman anointing Jesus, and in each case Jesus memorializes the woman's act as a holy gesture, coming from deep love for Him.

When Jesus was invited to dinner at the house of Simon the Pharisee, in the seventh chapter of Luke he says to Simon,

> 44 And he turned to the woman, and said unto Simon,
> Seest thou this woman? I entered into thine house, thou
> gavest me no water for my feet: but she hath washed my
> feet with tears, and wiped them with the hairs of her head.
> 45 Thou gavest me no kiss: but this woman since the time
> I came in hath not ceased to kiss my feet. 46 My head with
> oil thou didst not anoint: but this woman hath anointed

> my feet with ointment. [47] Wherefore I say unto thee, Her
> sins, which are many, are forgiven; for she loved much: but
> to whom little is forgiven, the same loveth little.

Thus, the first to stories featured women who were declared *heroines of faith* by the gospel writers. This story features a woman as a *heroine of love*, and thus, forgiven of many wrong-doings.

One of the most powerful examples is the conversation that Jesus has with the Samaritan woman at the well. This is recorded in *John* chapter 4. In this gospel story, the lady reacted with great surprise that Jesus, a Jew, would even approach and talk to her, a Samaritan and a woman. This was purely an evangelical act on the part of our Savior. He was trying to win human souls - PERIOD. He did not care if it was a male soul or a female soul.

The disciples were taken aback somewhat by this behavior. In *John* 4:27,

> [7] And upon this came his disciples, and marveled that he
> talked with the woman.

Walking up to this Samaritan lady was supposed to be a socially demeaning act for a Jewish adult male. Jesus didn't care. He did not see gender, nor did He see ethnicity in this person. He saw a human soul that He desired to set free.

Jesus Teaches on the Issue of Divorce

The elevation of women to a status equal to men comes not only from the way that Jesus treated women. It also is revealed in His teachings on social justice with regard to women. This takes its most common form in the teachings Jesus gave on the subject of divorce.

Before we get to far into what Jesus said about divorce regarding women, let us first examine an Old Testament passage to get a sense of where Jesus was coming from.

> *Malachi* 3:14,15

> *[14] Because the Lord hath been witness between thee and the wife of*

thy youth, against whom thou hast dealt treacherously: yet is she thy companion, and the wife of thy covenant. 15 And did not he make one? Yet had he the residue of the spirit. And wherefore one? That he might seek a godly seed. Therefore take heed to your spirit, and let none deal treacherously against the wife of his youth.

The book of Malachi was most likely written between 350 and 450 B.C., about a generation or two after the Jews returned from captivity in Babylon, and built the 2nd Temple. During this time women would have been nothing more than the property of their husbands. They had no rights during this time period to ask for a divorce if they were unhappy in their marriages. The husbands, on the other hand, could put them out in the street with a written letter of divorce on a mere whim. The anger of God's spirit against men, as seen in Malachi chapter 3, is on behalf of women who have been unfairly made homeless by divorce.

By the time of Jesus the situation for women is slightly better. In the first century if there were contractual terms in a marriage and the man broke those terms, if she could prove her case to a Jewish court, and the court ruled in her favor, they would put pressure on the man to write her a divorce letter. Thus, there was a painful first century process by which, under isolated circumstances, a woman could pursue a divorce. With this background, let us now look at an interesting conversation between Jesus and the Pharisees. From the 19th chapter of Matthew:

3 The Pharisees also came unto him, tempting him, and saying unto him, Is it lawful for a man to put away his wife for every cause? 4 And he answered and said unto them, Have ye not read, that he which made them at the beginning made them male and female, 5 And said, For this cause shall a man leave father and mother, and shall cleave to his wife: and they twain shall be one flesh? 6 Wherefore they are no more twain, but one flesh. What therefore God hath joined together, let not man put asunder. 7 They say unto him, Why did Moses then command to give a writing of divorcement, and to put her away? 8 He saith unto them, <u>Moses because of the hardness of your hearts suffered you to put away your wives: but from</u>

> *the beginning it was not so.* ⁹ *And I say unto you, Whosoever shall put away his wife, except it be for fornication, and shall marry another, committeth adultery: and whoso marrieth her which is put away doth commit adultery.*

Notice a few key points that Jesus is making here

1. The Torah scripture is not necessarily God - inspired, but it is more of Moses compromising with some very hard headed Israeli men.
2. God intended, from the beginning of the world, for couples to stay together.
3. In verse 9, two male behavioral choices are being mentioned: a) the man who divorced the woman, b) the man who marries a woman who was divorced by the first man.

Notice that in verse 9, the woman involved has not made any free will choices. The righteous judgment of Christ is solely directed at men in this passage.

This is an example of Jesus repeating a teaching that he had given earlier. Within the same gospel of Matthew, occurring much earlier in Matthew 5:31, Jesus is giving the Sermon on the Mount, and says,

> *31It hath been said, Whosoever shall put away his wife, let him give her a writing of divorcement: 32But I say unto you, That whosoever shall put away his wife, saving for the cause of fornication, causeth her to commit adultery: and whosoever shall marry her that is divorced committeth adultery.*

In this earlier version of the same teaching He says, **"causeth her to commit adultery"** - phrase that he does not use in his address to the Pharisees. In this teaching, He is still not talking about anything that was an act of free will choice on the part of the woman. Thus, the only possible meaning left to this phrase **"causeth her to commit adultery"** is that whatever the woman does *out of the economic necessity of survival,* her guilt is upon the man who put her in that situation by divorcing her. Logically, there can be no other meaning to the phrase. Later, in Mark 10:11-12, Jesus elevates the status of women by making them equally responsible under His new law concerning divorce:

> 11 And he saith unto them, Whosoever shall put away his wife, and marry another, committeth adultery against her. 12 And if a woman shall put away her husband, and be married to another, she committeth adultery.

In Mark 10:10-12, Jesus gives women a place of <u>equal responsibility</u> in the marriage relationship. Although it was much more difficult, in terms of legal procedure, for a woman to divorce a man in first century Judaism, it was possible, and Jesus made a great point here of acknowledging both equal power and equal responsibility for women, regarding His teachings on divorce.

The language in these verses is interesting and real in that each verse names the opposite gender spouse as the victim of the "divorce to marry another" act. Thus, Jesus implies here that the act of adultery involves much more personal harm than merely violating the property or territory rights of another man or woman. It acknowledges the personal injury that the adulterer does to his or her own spouse.

Remember the story in John 8:7 ? ***He that is without sin among you, let him first cast a stone at her.***

Here again, we see the evidence of the emphasis He places on the law being *equally applied* to both men and women. There is a very respectable and reliable scholarly tradition of interpretation that states, what He meant in context is "he that is without **THIS SIN** among you, let him cast the first stone". In other words, it is very likely that when Jesus was writing with his finger in the dirt before He stood up to speak, he was writing the names of the male adulterers who were now screaming for the woman's stoning.

Jesus Teaches Women

The above section title gets very little reaction from the modern reader. However, in the hearing of His fellow religious contemporaries this would have been scandalous news.

We can see quite plainly that Jesus did teach Mary and Martha the Torah and the Prophets of the Jewish Bible. At the resurrection of Lazarus, Martha makes mention of the prophecy of *Daniel*, concerning the resurrection at the final judgment.

There was a very common saying in the first century amongst Rabbis and Jewish priests -

> *it is better to burn the Torah in public than to teach it to a woman.*

Jesus did not care about this common social sentiment. He is determined to teach the word of His Father to all people regardless of gender.

The Double Standard of Roman Law and Paul's Teaching

In 1st century Roman society, a man *was not at all* considered to be guilty of marital unfaithfulness under Roman law if he

1. had sex with boy slaves, or any person of any age from the slave class
2. had sex with female or male prostitutes

In general, a married man could have intercourse with any person of a lower slave status and it was okay. Of course, the women during this time period had no such privilege, so there was an amazing double standard over what constituted adultery for men versus women in Roman society.

In contrast, Roman women could not have any kind of sex with anyone but their husband, and on their husband's terms.

Within the New Testament the Greek word *porneia* and its various forms is used twenty-five times. It is most interesting that Paul directs most of his uses of the word, most notably in 1 Corinthians chapters five(5) and six(6), at *men*, addressing immoral situations that *men* were largely the participants in.

Given the largely Gentile Greco-Roman cultures of Rome, Corinth, and Ephesus, Paul's position may have been surprising to his audience, which is all the more reason why he felt compelled to educate these men.

What will be most appreciated by modern day women who study Paul, is that, in contrast to common Roman high society, he had no double standard on the sexual morality as it would be applied to both men and women. One of his driving passions in the epistles was to let the men know that they were not off the hook on God's expectation that they be just as faithful to their wives, as their wives were to them.

Paul's Respect for Women and Their Leadership Contribution

There are several women mentioned by Paul as leaders and coworkers in the faith who deserve high esteem and regard. In his own letters, Paul does not appear to have any desire to limit their leadership activities, but instead he commends them and exhorts the church of Rome and other churches to receive them with great respect.   How does one make any sense of reconciling these passages with those where Paul appears to be putting women down?

There are a few explanations regarding passages where Paul seems to be saying to the women, "know your place, sit down, and shut up."   Most notoriously, these are 1 *Corinthians* 14:34-35 and 1 *Timothy* 3:8-13. For starters, most Bible scholars believe, based on simple literary and historical analysis that 1 *Timothy* was written 80 years after Paul in the 2nd century, but attributed to him. As for 1 *Corinthians* 14, there are two commonly known possibilities. One possibility is that Paul was addressing a very specific situation at the church of Corinth. This was actually a pattern in Paul's epistle writing. Another possibility is that marginal notes were mistaken as main content by the scribal workers who made copies of original manuscripts. These explanations of 1 *Corinthians* 14:34-35 must be sought on the grounds that without them, the epistle of 1 *Corinthians* contradicts itself. In 1 *Corinthians* 11:5, Paul assumes without objection that women will pray and prophesy openly within the church.

The story on Paul's attitudes towards women would not be complete without mentioning four(4) female church leaders that he had the utmost respect for - Priscilla, Phoebe, Lydia, and Chloe.

In *Romans* 16:3-4, Paul writes,

> *Greet Priscilla and Aquila, my co-workers in Christ Jesus, who risked their necks for my life, to whom not only I am grateful but also all the churches of the Gentiles....*

Priscilla and her husband Aquila were Roman refugees in Corinth who had been forced to leave then the emperor expelled the Jews from Rome. In writing the churches of Rome, Paul acknowledges that this couple put their lives on the line for him, risking their necks. This couple led a church home group at Corinth. This is acknowledged in 1 *Corinthians* 16:19 -

> *The churches of Asia salute you. Aquila and Priscilla salute you much in the Lord, with the church that is in their house.*

With many other similar references, it is very plan that Paul saw these people as his apostolic equals, and Priscilla's usually mentioned first, implying that she was very likely the more prominent leadership figure in the couple. Paul commends another woman in *Romans* 16:1-2 who was a leader in the region of Corinth.

> *I commend to you Phoebe our sister, who is a minister of the Church at Cenchreae, that you may receive her in the Lord in a manner worthy of the holy ones, and help her in whatever she may need from you, for she has been a benefactor to many and to me as well.*

The word "minister" here comes from the Greek word **diakonos,** which means "deacon". The concept of a deacon saw much change and evolution over the first 100 years after Paul. What would always be similar at any period of church history is that **diakonos** has been an esteemed position of church leadership. Paul's reference to Phoebe is in the form of a letter of recommendation so that she will be welcomed with hospitality when she reaches the Christian community in Rome. There is an implication here that in her official role she functioned in a missionary capacity with occasional travel required.

Chloe held the function of being the eyes and ears of Paul in Corinth while he was away on other missions. This is made very apparent by *Corinthians* 1:10-11

> *10 Now I beseech you, brethren, by the name of our Lord Jesus Christ, that ye all speak the same thing, and that there be no divisions among you; but that ye be perfectly joined together in the same mind and in the same judgment. 11 For it hath been declared unto me of you, my brethren, by them which are of the house of Chloe,*

that there are contentions among you.

There is a subtle implication in "then which are of the house of Chloe" that she lead a home church group.

Paul's first Gentile convert was Lydia, who is described in the book of Acts as a dealer in purple fabrics. As these were expensive goods, she is taken in context to have been a lady of great wealth.

She urged Paul to be a guest in her house, and the implication is that she later became host to a home church.

In our next chapter, we will deal with a topic that will be challenging for most Christians: what the Bible really says about homosexuality. What will be of equal importance in the message of the next chapter is what the Bible *is not saying* about homosexuality.

4 HOMOSEXUALITY: WHAT THE BIBLE REALLY SAYS ABOUT IT

This chapter delivers an in depth analysis of passages in the Bible that *appear* to deal with the subject of homosexuality. These are the passages most quoted and used in Bible commentary today to say that homosexuality is a specialized type of sexual sin.

This book will deal with the New Testament passages first from the KJV. There are three of these passage in the New Testament and three in the Old Testament.

The first and most well-known passage is in the first chapter of *Romans*. The second New Testament passage is in *1 Corinthians 6:9-10,* and the 3rd passage in the New Testament is *1 Timothy 1:9,10*. Both of these last two New Testament passages in the KJV have the mysterious phrase "abusers of themselves with mankind". As we dig deeper into the historical usage of Greek, we will learn much more about the true meaning of the Greek word that this phrase comes from.

For the remaining three areas that are heavily quoted from in the Old Testament, they are *Leviticus 20:13, Leviticus 18:22*, and of course the Sodom and Gomorrah story in *Genesis*. The discussion of these scriptures will be in relation to the New Testament passages that reference them indirectly.

In the analysis of each of these passages, we will first acknowledge the meaning and interpretations that our modern day church culture gives to these passages. Immediately after that, <u>we will study historical and cultural contexts of the communities that produced these scriptures, to arrive at what these passages meant to 1st century Greco-Roman and Hellenistic audiences.</u>

We will also look at what certain words and concepts meant to the generation that produced these scriptures, and we will compare how those words and concepts were used in other bodies of literature produced <u>within that very same time period and culture.</u> It is from such analysis that we are most likely to arrive at the *originally intended meaning* of a passage of scripture.

The First Chapter of Romans

Our first survey point of homosexuality in the New Testament is Romans chapter 1. In actuality, it is important to get a the very heart of what Paul was trying to communicate to the Roman church by going a little bit further into the first few verses of chapter 2. It is only by going this far that we can truly see the broader context of Paul's message.

From the KJV, the passage reads as follows :

> *26 For this cause God gave them up unto vile affections: for even their women did change the natural use into that which is against nature:*

> *27 And likewise also the men, leaving the natural use of the woman, burned in their lust one toward another; men with men working that which is unseemly, and receiving in themselves that recompense of their error which was meet*

If we read the verse just before verse 26, we see that there is a context for this event of human behavior that is being described. The use of past tense verbs in these two verses makes it quite clear that Paul is referring to something that has happened already as a part of a known history. Verses 23 - 25 read:

> *23 And changed the glory of the uncorruptible God into an image made like to corruptible man, and to birds, and four footed beasts, and creeping things.*

> *24 Wherefore God also gave them up to uncleanness through the lusts of their own hearts, to dishonor their own bodies between themselves:*

> *25 Who changed the truth of God into a lie, and worshiped and served the creature more than the Creator, who is blessed for ever. Amen*

Thus, we see from the surrounding verses that "God gave them up" to these "vile" affections. In modern day language, we would say that God allowed them to develop sexual addictions that eventually became perversions away from the norm. Why did God allow this? The context makes it clear that it was a natural consequence of spiritual idolatry.

If we look at the historical context of this passage, we can also see that there is indeed a historical phenomenon of human behavior that Paul is trying to address in the context of pagan idol worship. In 186 B.C. the Roman historian Livy unveiled the practice of homosexual initiation of young men in the rites of Bacchus. These young men were not necessarily of a natural homosexual leaning, but from repeated exposure during these rites did become that way. Thus, "God gave them up unto vile affections", so the wording of the scripture itself talks about someone who has **crossed over** from heterosexuality to homosexuality, and that it was <u>specifically taking place in the context of pagan ritual orgies.</u>

The rites were highly secretive because there was a strong aversion within Roman society to the idea of a man taking a subservient sexual role to receive penetration. Living in the generation just before Paul, Roman Historian Livy was basically blowing the lid on a secret scandal of his generation. The Greek word translated "vile" in this KJV passage literally means "dishonorable". This is a cultural reference to the shame that existed in Roman society for an adult male who assumed the position of a woman during sex. This Bacchus pagan initiation practice - where young heterosexual adults were forced into homosexual acts - continued in secret well beyond the life of the Apostle Paul.

In the broader context of chapter 1, from verse 26 through the end of the chapter, Paul gives a long list of carnal activities on the part of Gentile people which starts with idolatry being the root sin leading to the degenerative process of declining morals. <u>Paul concludes that the whole world is under this influence, and that in one way or another, we are all guilty of some form of idolatry and carnal degeneration.</u> This brings us to Paul's broader contextual message. The 2nd chapter of *Romans* begins with this verse:

> *1 Therefore thou art inexcusable, O man, whosoever thou art that judgest: for wherein thou judgest another, thou condemnest thyself; for*

thou that judgest doest the same things.

2 But we are sure that the judgment of God is according to truth against them which commit such things.

So, for those of us who have a tendency to read from *Romans* 1:26 and 27, while confronting a homosexual person in the church with it to tell them that they are going to Hell, we probably should heed the broader context of Paul's message. **God alone is qualified to judge another human being. Its not our job.**

It is very interesting to note that the wording of these verses specifically calls out those people who started their life as heterosexuals. In Paul's use of phrases like "burned in their lust" indicates that these are not long term human commitments (i.e., lifetime committments, such as we find in same sex marriage) serving as the context for the same-sex behaviors. In fact these heterosexuals became so wanton with lust in the extreme, that they crossed over into homosexual behaviors when it was not their natural sexual orientation.

Why were their lusts degenerating and changing into something that they were not born with? The context in *Romans* 1 says it was because of idolatry. In their carnal rage they sought to experiment with every sexual expression under the sun, and pagan ritualistic orgy would have been the perfect setting for that.

What about those individuals who have honestly reported to us that from the onset of early adolescence and puberty they have never once been attracted to an opposite gender person? For this particular group of homosexuals, if we are going to take the wording of *Romans* 1:26 and 27 as *word-for-word literal*, it is logical to say that this particular group of homosexuals is not even being addressed by the Bible. For those readers who say, "Just wait till you see n *1 Corinthians 6:9-10,* and *1 Timothy 1:9,10."*, please fasten your seat belts because we are going there in the next chapters of this book.

The "Effeminate" Corinthians

The epistle to the Corinthians from the KJV brings out the word "effeminate" in its translation, and this word has been linked in many commentaries to homosexuality. The scripture under consideration is *1 Corinthians 6:9-10*:

> *9 Know ye not that the unrighteous shall not inherit the kingdom of God? Be not deceived: neither fornicators, nor idolaters, nor adulterers, nor* **effeminate***, nor abusers of themselves with mankind,*

> *10 Nor thieves, nor covetous, nor drunkards, nor revilers, nor extortioners, shall inherit the kingdom of God.*

The Greek word is **malakos** and it is used in many other Greek writings of the time period to mean "soft" in a pleasure seeking way, without will power or self control.

This same word - **malakos** - is used by Jesus in Matthew 11:8 when he is describing John the Baptist.

> *But what went ye out for to see? A man clothed in soft (**malakos**) raiment? behold, they that wear soft clothing are in kings' houses.*

Of course, in this question about John, Jesus was making a veiled reference to Herod, a man who did where soft robes and live in a palace.

This word had some literary history by the time of Jesus. Some 350 years before Christ, Aristotle talks about the concept of the **malakos** in his "Nicomachean Ethics".

> "of the dispositions described above, the deliberate avoidance of pain is rather a kind of softness (malakia); the deliberate pursuit of pleasure is profligacy in the strict sense.";

> "One who is deficient in resistance to pains that most men withstand with success, is soft (malakos) or luxurious, for luxury is a kind of softness (malakia); such a man lets his cloak trail on the ground to escape the fatigue and trouble

of lifting it, or feigns sickness, not seeing that to counterfeit misery is to be miserable."

— Nicomachean Ethics, Loeb vol 73, VII vii 7; pg 417

The logical conclusion that we must draw about the "effeminate" is that this word, in the way that this scripture is often quoted and used, <u>does not really appear in the New Testament</u>.

As we have seen from the explanations and examples above, phrase "soft with self indulgence" is a much more accurate translation of *malakos*. If a homosexually effeminate man was meant by this verse of scripture, Paul would have used the word **kinaidos, which was the common Greek term used in Paul's generation for an effeminate homosexual male.**

There is another term in this passage that the KJV translates "abusers of themselves with mankind". This word is *arsenokoitai*, a term that does not appear in the history of the written Greek language before it is first used by the Apostle Paul in his letters. Paul is actually making up a word concept out of two words - *arseno*, which means man, and *koitai* which means "put to bed". Thus, a most direct translation in Paul's usage would be *man-bedder*. We will refrain from explaining more about what Paul really meant by this term until we get to Paul's use of *arsenokoitai* in *1 Timothy 1:9,10*. After this book's analysis of that passage, it will be come very clear what Paul meant by *man-bedder*.

There are many Bible translations of *arsenokoitai* that translate it into English as either *homosexual* or *sodomite*. In the chapters that follow, we are about to demonstrate that those translations of "man-bedder" are likely to be incorrect.

For starters, the Greek language of Paul's generation had many well-known words for homosexuality. These words appear in the Greek texts of Philo and Josephus, and many earlier Greek writers. The word *paiderasste* was a very general Greek term for homosexuality, and as a general term, it would have been the direct equivalent of just saying "homosexual" in modern English. The word **lakkoproktoi was used to denote anal penetration.**

As we have seen earlier, *kinaidos* was used to denote an effeminate homosexual. The word for transvestite was *euryproktoi*, and *dihetaristriai* was the term for a lesbian. This is just scratching the surface on many of the words that Paul could have used from the Greek language of his time period.

Thus, it is logical to conclude that if Paul was meaning to describe homosexuality as we know it today, there are many other more suitable and appropriate Greek words that he would have used.   With this being the case, it behooves us to understand just what it was the Paul was referring to.

The two words that ***arsenokoitai*** comes from actually appear in the Greek Septuagint version of *Leviticus 20:13* and also *Leviticus 18:22*. The verse prohibits a man who lies with a man as one would normally lie with a woman. The average reader at this point would say "Aha! It's talking about gay men", but the point of Paul using that term and not using the word ***paiderasste*** is that the Torah was talking about ***homosexual acts within a certain context***, and not a general condemnation of homosexuality.

Admittedly, most orthodox rabbinical commentaries on *Leviticus 20:13* and *Leviticus 18:22* do say that these moral codes were intended to stand on their own, regardless of why they were originally instituted. The Reform denominations of Judaism, however, say that the original reasons for institution *mean everything*, when we are deciding whether or not the edict should apply in our modern times.

There is a reference to a pagan deity called Molech in *Leviticus 18:21*. According the Documentary Hypothesis - a scholarly theory about how the Torah was put together over time - most of Leviticus came from the Priestly Source. There is a general consensus among Bible scholars that the Holiness Code of *Leviticus* - chapters 17 to 26 - was later added to the original Priestly Source material of *Leviticus*, and this section was probably appended in the seventh century before Christ. This would explain why there are five(5) references to Molech in the Holiness Code section of *Leviticus*. During this time period there was heavy religious competition between the priests of the Lord and the priests of Molech. Most of the sexual prohibitions mentioned in chapters 18 and 20 are specific to acts being performed during ritual orgies to Molech and Ashtoreth. Thus, the homosexual acts mentioned are in a <u>pagan idol worship context,</u> along with many other acts, such as incest and bestiality that were also part of those pagan orgies.

From a historical commentary on *2 Kings 23:7*, *The Interpreter's Dictionary of the Bible* states

> *"Fertility rites were practiced at the numerous shrines which dotted the land, as well as at the major sanctuaries... A characteristic feature of the fertility cult was sacral sexual intercourse by priests and priestesses and other specially consecrated persons, sacred prostitutes* **<u>of both sexes</u>*... **Child-sacrifice was also a feature of the rites..."***

> - The Interpreter's Dictionary of The Bible, Volume 3, Abingdon, 1990, pages 933-934.

In *Leviticus 18:21,* the verse just before the first prohibition against "man lying with man", there is a prohibition against child sacrifice to Molech. The commentary above from *he Interpreter's Dictionary of the Bible* makes it very clear that **the context of this human behavior is the child sacrifice and the ritual sex occurred within the very same rite**. Thus, it could be logically implied that this passage in *Leviticus* is addressing a human behavior that has nothing to do with modern day, consensual, same-sex relationships.

These same pagan orgies to false gods were still going on during the life of the Apostle Paul, with the cult of Bacchus-Dionysus being well known in the early Roman world for its homosexual initiation rites. The donation of slave boys as temple prostitutes by the pagan wealthy was also a well-known practice.

There is a religious debate even within denominations of Judaism on this issue. The Orthodox sects say that the original reason or context for the homosexual act - pagan idol worship - does not matter. The moral code should stand on its own regardless, says the Orthodox Jew. The Reform Jew, on the other hand, says that the reason for something being a sin does matter, <u>especially if that reason or situation does not exist today</u>. **One**

thing that both Reform and Orthodox commentaries for *Leviticus* agree on is that this was a collection of sexual acts <u>that were specifically part of a pagan idol worship rite or ceremony.</u>

These pagan rituals were causing otherwise heterosexual men to take on homosexual acts upon themselves - all in the name of worshiping Molech. The mandate from *Leviticus* 18 and 20 had more to do with outlawing a few bizarre practices that had been introduced as pagan Canaanite worship. Outside of a pagan ritual context, it is fair to say that the Bible isn't speaking that specifically to human sexual behavior, other than to outlaw various forms of adultery.

Here is one very curious question. If a moral law against homosexuality is being established in *Leviticus*, <u>why is there no specific prohibition mentioned about a woman lying with a woman?</u>

In the Canaanite nations, a male temple prostitute would often assume the submissive female position. In a patriarchal society it would be this aspect of "dominating a male in the way that you would a woman" that was found to be offensive. <u>The same-sex nature of the sexual encounter would not be reason for its prohibition. The reason was than man was seen as superior, made in God's image, and it is a disgrace for him to be dominated sexually.</u> If our hypothesis is wrong, **then there would have been a scripture in *Leviticus* prohibiting lesbian sex.** We could also go on about other reasons for the edict that would not at all be relevant for modern times, such as the need for Israel to increase the size of its population.

Analysis of Arsenokoitai in 1 Timothy

The mysterious phrase "man bedder" will not be so mysterious after the scriptural analysis presented in this chapter. There is a strong parallel of meaning and message between the words of *1 Timothy 1:9,10* and the ten commandments given in *Exodus*. Here is the passage under consideration:

> *9 Knowing this, that the law is not made for a righteous man, but for the lawless and disobedient, for the ungodly and for sinners, for unholy and profane, for murderers of fathers and murderers of mothers, for manslayers,*

10 For whoremongers, for them that defile themselves with mankind, for menstealers, for liars, for perjured persons, and if there be any other thing that is contrary to sound doctrine;

As we start to line this up with the Ten Commandments we have:

Thou shalt have no other gods before me	the lawless and disobedient
Thou shalt not make unto thee any graven image	the ungodly and sinners
Thou shalt not take the name of the Lord thy God in vain	the profane
Remember the Sabbath day, to keep it holy	the unholy
Honor thy father and thy mother	murderers of fathers and murderers of mothers
Thou shalt not kill	man-slayers
Thou shalt not commit adultery	whoremongers, them that defile themselve with mankind
Thou shalt not steal	men-stealers
Thou shalt not bear false witness against thy neighbor	liars, perjurers
Thou shalt not covet	whatever else is contrary to sound doctrine

The first two of these are not a dead on match, but starting with the 3rd commandment there is a perfect alignment. It is very likely that Paul was attempting to deliver the moral code of the ten commandments to Gentile Christians in this epistle, except that a few noteworthy clarifications are delivered as well.

The list of moral codes from *1 Timothy 1:9,10* is very similar to another teaching given in the 2nd chapter of the *Didache* in the first century. The *Didache* was a 1st century body of teaching meant for Christians of Greek and Roman culture to clarify the ten commandments and other facets of proper Judeo Christian ethic.

In 1st century Roman society, a man was not at all considered to be guilty of marital unfaithfulness under Roman law if he

1. had sex with boy slaves, or any person of any age from the slave class
2. had sex with female or male prostitutes

In general, a married man could have intercourse with any person of a lower slave status and it was okay. Of course, the women during this time period had no such privilege, so there was an amazing double standard over what constituted adultery for men versus women in Roman society.

From the earliest Roman periods, it was perfectly normal, legal, and acceptable for an older man to desire and pursue young boys. However, children of free Roman citizens were off limits under Roman law. For slaves there was no protection under the law even against rape.

Given the highly populated, high society metropolitan environments of Corinth, Ephesus, and Rome, it is well within the realm of possibility that at least some older men - already possessing young boy sex slaves - were converting to Christianity in the 1st century. Thus, without instructions from the Apostle Paul, and also from other 1st century writings such as *Didache* and the *Epistle of Barnabus*, a Greek and Roman segment of the church may have had no way of knowing that this was wrong.

The Jews were seen as puritanical and even prudish by the rest of the civilized world as revealed by this abstract from the *Sibylline Oracles*:

> *[The Jews] are mindful of holy wedlock,*
>
> *and they do not engage in impious intercourse with male children,*
>
> *as do Phoenicians, Egyptians and Romans,*
>
> *spacious Greece and many nations of other,*

Persians and Galatians and all Asia, transgressing

the holy law of immortal God, which they transgressed

This translated passage of the *Sibylline Oracles* is taken from "*Where is boasting?*" by Simon J. Gathercole, page 175.

The only sexual moral code from *Exodus* chapter 20 was "you will not commit adultery", and for Romans the definition of adultery <u>was very different from the Jewish definition</u>. Thus, in the *Didache*, the *Epistle of Barnabas*, and *1 Timothy 1:9,10*, a **<u>certain stand had to be taken to extend and enhance the moral codes on adultery</u>**. For this group of new Christians, merely saying, "you will not commit adultery" was not enough.

Just before the word ***arsenokoitai*** in verse 10 is the word ***pornos*** (translated "whoremonger" in the KJV), and this word ***pornos*** is very interesting in the way that it is used elsewhere in the New Testament. The literal definition of ***pornos***, taken from *Strong's Concordance* (Greek word #4205) is

> 4205 pórnos (from pernaō, "to sell off") – properly, a male prostitute. 4205 (pórnos) is "properly, 'a male prostitute' ;

The word shares the same root form as ***porneia***, which is the general term translated as fornication or promiscuity in the New Testament (also from which our word "pornography" comes from).

Although, its literal definition is "male prostitute", in *Hebrews* chapter 12 ***pornos*** is used in recounting a story about Esau, who, according to Jewish tradition seduced and raped the wives of another man just moments after selling his birthright to Jacob for a delicious meal. Likewise, in *1 Corinthians 5:1* ***pornos*** is translated "fornication" in the KJV, and it is used of a man who commits adultery with his father's wife. In other parts of the New Testament, it falls into a generic "carnal nature" list, or otherwise a list intended to parallel the ten commandments of *Exodus* chapter 20 in the way that *1 Timothy 1:9,10* does.

In the case of *1 Timothy*, it is then very appropriate for ***pornos*** (whoremonger) to be lined up with "you will not commit adultery", because in other New Testament places, an act of adultery is exactly how the word is being used. When one takes into account the expansion of Gentile Christian moral codes on the subject of adultery, as mentioned in the 1st century works, *Didache*, and the *Epistle of Barnabas*, the KJV's translation to "whoremonger" is most appropriate.

When both *Didache* and the *Epistle of Barnabas* start to roll out their versions of the ten commandments for Gentile Christians, they very interestingly mention a list of three prohibitions,

- do not have sex with prostitutes,
- do not have sex with a married woman,
- do not commit pederasty (sex with boy slaves)

as an expanded replacement of the single commandment, "do not commit adultery".

Of course, where we are going with this is that the use of ***arsenokoitai***, the word following ***pornos***, is an out spoken condemnation of the "man bedders" - a term we are about to give some definition to.

Our other revealing factor about ***pornos*** and ***arsenokoitai*** has to do with how the words of *1 Timothy 1:9,10* are logically grouped within the entire two verse passage. The first two terms are *lawless* and *disobedient.* In a very real sense the words almost carry the same implication. Likewise, consider the next two groups *ungodly* and *sinners*, and then *profane* and *unholy*.

A patterns starts to emerge in the grouping of words in verses 9 and 10. The pattern is one of either similar or otherwise closely related meaning. The words in a word group are very close to being synonyms of each other. The next word group "murderers of fathers and murderers of mothers, for man-slayers" is obviously taking about that murderous, killing type of person, with the first two also being related to the *Exodus* command to honor our parents.

Before we look at a word group in the middle that we are really interested in, notice the last word group, *liars* and *perjurers*. This leaves the final word group that we skipped expressed as

"whoremongers, them that defile themselves with mankind, men-stealers".

Let us now look at how these three words appear in the original Greek .

- *pornos* - male prostitute,
- *arsenokoitai* - "man bedders"
- *andrapodistēs* - kidnapper, slave trader

In keeping with this logical analysis approach, all other groupings of words in *1 Timothy 1:9,10* were of closely related meaning. Some of the word groups were very near being synonyms of each other. At first, 3rd bullet may not seem to fit with the group, but if you take into account the historical fact that most prostitutes within the 1st century Roman empire were of a slavery status, the 3rd bullet fits rather nicely.

In this next paragraph, we will give slight situational expansion to the meaning of each term, but we will do so while still using the translated terms.

- *pornos* - Male Prostitutes, who were first **kidnapped into slavery as children**, and then subjected to **continual rape by the *arsenokoitai***, eventually causing them to remain as male prostitutes (***pornos***) well into adulthood
- *arsenokoitai* - Those "man bedders" who sexually rape and "own" the young slave boys, well into their adulthood
- *andrapodistēs* - The kidnapper or slave trader, who can **legally kidnap any young boy** coming from a non-Roman conquered race of people, and sell the boy into slavery

All three words, in this rendering, are grouped together and related by way of describing the set of crimes involved in the human trafficking of young boys as sex slaves. To the secular society of Rome, these things were acceptable. Paul had to make a point to his Gentile Church that within the Christian family these things were NOT acceptable.

Thus, from the analysis above it should be easy to conclude that Paul was not at all talking about condemnation of same-sex adult relationships as they exist today.

Although pederasty was specifically condemned in the *Didache* and the *Epistle of Barnabas*, these 1st century works are not the in the authoritative cannon of scripture. Scripture from the cannon must have spoken out on this, and *1 Corinthians 6:9-10* and *1 Timothy 1:9,10* are the only possible candidates for carrying this message.

There is another implication of **arsenokoitai** which relates back to the passage in the first chapter of *Romans* that we talked about earlier.

The boy sex slave was often donated to a temple cult, after which he was castrated and forced to serve as a sacral prostitute providing anal sex. Justin Martyr, and early church father who lived from 100 - 165 A.D. reports on these events.

> *"And there are some who prostitute even their own children and wives, and some are openly mutilated for the purpose of sodomy; and they refer these mysteries to the mother of the gods"*

> - Justin Martyr, First Apology, 27.

The term "mother of the gods" in Justin's report is a reference to Cybele. The worship of Cybele using castrated young male slaves for ritual sex was widespread throughout the Roman empire.

Given what we know about **arsenokoitai,** the "man bedder" in the Apostle Paul's writing is referring to those men who take advantage of these young boy temple prostitutes. At the same time, within Roman society, there were men engaged in **paiderasste** who were in a free and consensual relationship with each other.   <u>It does not take a rocket scientist in the field of ethics to see that these were completely different moral contexts for a homosexual act.</u> The **arsenokoitai** is continually raping a child slave, while **paiderasste** is a free act between consenting adults. The same-sex relationship that we know of in our modern era is not the kind of sex that the "man bedders" were having.

Our modern day same-sex marriage is a form of homosexual relationship that the New Testament is completely silent on. If that were not the case, the word *paiderasste* would be appearing as a Greek word in our New Testament.

By making these statements, the author is **not** saying necessarily that general homosexuality (*paiderasste)* is **not** a sin. (Let God alone be the judge of that, in any given situation where human sexuality is involved.) The only case being laid here is the Bible scriptures themselves do not single out homosexuality (*paiderasste)* as being a sin.

A Return Sodom

Everything seems to start with this story in Genesis that talks about a few cities that are being wiped off the map by God's wrath. The term "sodomite" or terms like "sodomy" link homosexual acts directly to Sodom. This deeper look into scriptural references to Sodom throughout the Bible shows that homosexuality was not the reason they provoked God to wrath. Sodom's judgment and example are also mentioned in *Jeremiah 23:14*, *Isaiah 1:10-17*, and *Zephaniah 2:8-11*. These passages talk about the injustice, brutality, and oppression of Sodom towards its visitors and its neighbors, but <u>nothing at all is said about its homosexuality</u>.

Concerning those cities who refuse to receive the disciples of Jesus, he said in *Matthew 10:14-15*,

> ***14 And whosoever shall not receive you, nor hear your words, when ye depart out of that house or city, shake off the dust of your feet.***
>
> ***15 Verily I say unto you, It shall be more tolerable for the land of Sodom and Gomorrha in the day of judgment, than for that city.***

There is a common thread here in what Jesus is saying, and in the Genesis story of Sodom - *a lack of hospitality*, a cultural crime of great insult in the middle east. It is implied in his statement that the lack of hospitality is what brought God's wrath to them.

In demanding to gang rape Lot's house guests, Sodom was showing a lack of hospitality in the most brutal and violent way. We can infer from what the angel's told Lot that the violence of the city was one of the key reasons that they had come to destroy the place. The word "violence" is not used directly, but it is implied from *Genesis 19:13*

> **13 For we are about to destroy this place, because the outcry against its people has become great before the LORD, and the LORD has sent us to destroy it**

In order to understand how extreme violence is being implied here, it is necessary to be aware of the use of language in the extra-Biblical literature coming from the same historical period and culture.

The phrase "outcry against its people has become great before the LORD" is a pattern of language that also appears in the *Book of Enoch*. In Enoch, the sons of fallen angels - the giants - were killing, raping, and even eating people. These giants became kings and rulers who also had to power to abuse everyone they wanted to abuse. In Enoch it was the archangels, such as Michael, who brought to the attention of God the outcry of men who suffered violence, and the flow of blood that was taking place in the earth.

Both *Genesis* and *Enoch* are believed by scholars to have been written in roughly the same time period. The entire story within the *Book of Enoch* is essentially the detail expansion of what happens in *Genesis* chapter 6. The use of the same pattern of language would indicate that the men of Sodom were violent brutes, much like the giants from *Enoch*.

The logical conclusion to all of this is that our modern religious culture and tradition has caused many of us to see and interpret that homosexuality is the reason why God reigned down fire upon Sodom. If one looks at **ALL** scripture references to Sodom, and what they **ALL** say about why Sodom was judged, it becomes very obvious that homosexuality had little to do with why God wiped out an entire city.

5 CONCLUSIONS: A SCRIPTURAL BASIS FOR PROGRESSIVE THEOLOGY

In our introductory chapter, we have seen numerous examples in the Bible that contradicted and completely reversed Bible passages that were written earlier in history.

Of all the issues we have examined, the Bible's position on divorce is what has changed the most. The Old Testament prophets of the Jewish Bible seem to overturn the divorce law long before Jesus arrives on the scene.

There have been other behaviors on the part of Jesus and his disciples regarding Torah laws of ritual purity and kosher dietary laws, that would seem to indicate that neither Jesus, nor his disciples had much regard for these works of scripture.

It is the author's hope that fundamentalist Christians reading this book will start to be just a little bit more open minded about treating the Bible as a book that is not completely perfect or consistent in its written message.

Divine inspiration should take on a meaning that has more to do with the LOVE message of God as the scriptures and Bible stories express it, and its meaning should have less to do with concepts such as **infallibility** and **inerrancy** of mere words written down by humans.

In our second chapter we boldly questioned the very existence of Hell, and we used the original Greek language, combined with the early Church History of how the philosophies if Plato invaded our religion, so that punishment could be **eternally suffered** at the hands of a much more cruel version of the one true God. While the eternal punishment is not necessarily supported by the original Greek New Testament, the concept of divine consequence most certainly is - per the law of sowing and reaping.

The idea of a consequence being "eternal" is what we cannot find in the Greek sentences that were translated to contain "Hell" as an English word. We also saw how the word for "Hell" was the name of a burning garbage dump to the south and southwest of Mount Zion.

We have seen how that the word translated to "eternity" or "everlasting" comes from a Greek word - *aion* - that had no equivalent concept of this when used as a single Greek adjective.

After looking at the actual Greek context of these words, we came to discuss how the concept of eternity really did enter our Christian religion - through the influence of Plato on our early church fathers. <u>Thus, our common Christian belief in eternity for the human soul actually comes from Platonic Metaphysics, and has no original source in the Greek New Testament.</u>

In our third chapter, we saw how the New Testament actually promoted the ideas of gender equality in the society of that time period. In this journey we have seen the level of respect that Jesus demonstrated in His dealings with women. In situations where the female personality was demonstrating unparalleled levels of either faith or love, Jesus was completely gender-blind. In those circumstances, He could have cared less what the social observers around Him thought concerning his interactions with these women of faith and love.

We have also seen that in the view of divorce that Jesus has, men and women are of equal status, and that wives are not property, but female images of the one true God, and equal to men in matters of justice.

We have also seen shocking evidence of how the human sexuality teachings of the Apostle Paul were actually far reaching attempts on his part to equalize the status of women for Christians living under Roman social norms that disrespected women. We also see that contrary to church traditions about Paul that are based on 1 Timothy 2:11-15, Paul was not against women having leadership or teaching positions in the church on a universal level *for all time*. In the history of the church, we have been very good at taking the messages of Paul that were meant to address a very specific situation within a very specific church, and then trying to make some universal theology out of it, when that was what neither Paul, nor the

Holy Spirit necessarily intended. Thus, is the nature of how human traditions and cultural bias have a contribution to the formation of traditional theology itself. To show that this was not a universal view on the part of the Apostle Paul, there is plenty of evidence given to us in scriptures throughout the New Testament, which we have already discussed in the 3rd chapter.

Finally, in our last chapter we dealt with the most controversial issue debated by Christian Conservatives and Progressives - homosexuality and the Bible. In the first chapter of Romans, we see Paul's general criticism of the carnal, self-indulging ways of the Gentiles. We also see a group of heterosexual men and women crossing the boundary of their natural comfort zone into homosexual behavior, with the initial motivation being the ritual orgies of a pagan deity.

We also see how the historical record backs up this hypothesis and point to what Paul is actually referring to. In 186 B.C. the Roman historian Livy unveiled the practice of homosexual initiation of young men in the rites of Bacchus. These young men were not necessarily of a natural homosexual leaning, but from repeated exposure during these rites did become that way. Thus, "God gave them up unto vile affections", so the wording of the scripture itself talks about someone who has **crossed over** from heterosexuality to homosexuality, and that it was <u>specifically taking place in the context of pagan ritual orgies.</u>

In *1 Corinthians 6:9-10,* we saw that the meaning of **malakos** is "soft" in a pleasure seeking way, without will power or self control. Writings of Aristotle and even the use of the word in Christ's teaching confirm this more accurate translation. If a homosexually effeminate man was meant by this verse of scripture, Paul would have used the word **kinaidos, which was the common Greek term used in Paul's generation for an effeminate homosexual male.**

Both *1 Corinthians 6:9-10,* and *1 Timothy 1:9,10* contain "abusers of themselves with mankind", which comes from the word **arsenokoitai.** We explored various clues from different areas of context to get at a more accurate meaning of this term. First of all we showed that Paul made this word up, and that this word play came from the Greek Septuagint version of *Leviticus 20:13* and also *Leviticus 18:22*. We saw how the Holiness Code section of *Leviticus* was written later to support the priests of the one true God in a written polemic against the priests of Molech and Ashtoreth, the cults of whom required temple prostitution and ritual orgies involving temple prostitutes. We also shared the historical record, with some of that coming from early church father testimony, to the effect that temple prostitution and sacred orgies involving homosexual acts were still going on in Paul's generation. This is why a veiled reference to a concept in Leviticus by Paul was extremely appropriate.

We made note of the fact that the word **paiderasste** was a well known Greek word in Paul's generation for homosexual adult men having a consensual and committed relationship - completely outside of pagan temple involvement. This was the word for general homosexuality during Paul's lifetime. If he had sought to condemn <u>all homosexuals</u>, he would have simply used the word. According to the actual Greek words used, and the historical context of the period, Paul is only speaking out against adultery, sex with temple prostitutes, and raping boys.

Lastly, we took another look at Sodom, and this time we reviewed all of the other passages where Sodom is mentioned, and what these passages actually say about what Sodom was judged for. In summary, we found that the fire from heaven came for reasons other than homosexual acts.

We will close this book with the following thoughts.

Given what was presented, analyzed, and reviewed in this book, are we 100% sure about the judgments we make about homosexuality?

Admittedly, there is always the general case for sexual sin, which is culturally understood by most world religions as sexual intimacy outside of the context of marriage. Even if we have clearly demonstrated that the Bible *does not* single out <u>general homosexuality</u> (not connected to prostitution or pagan worship) as a specific type of sexual sin, fornication is loosely defined as ANY sex between two non-married persons. Of course, the legality of same sex marriage in several states of the United States, per a recent Supreme Court ruling is starting to muddy the water a little on that basis for judgment. (The old saying "Sex outside of wedlock = fornication")

It is the opinion of the author that the Bible is actually silent on the topic of homosexual relationships as they exist in our modern world.

Let God alone be the judge.

John Humble

REFERENCES

Thomas B Thayer - *The Origin and History of the Doctrine of Endless Punishment.* Boston: Universalist Pub. House, 1855.

Encyclopedia Britannica, s.V. "Athenagoras", 11th ed., 831

Dr. LeRoy E Froom, *Conditionalist Faith of Our Fathers* [1965], vol. 1, p. 954

Nicomachean Ethics, Loeb vol 73, VII vii 7; pg 417

The Interpreter's Dictionary of The Bible, Volume 3, Abingdon, 1990, pages 933-934.

Strong, James. Strong's Exhaustive Concordance of the Bible. Abingdon Press, 1890. Print.

ABOUT THE AUTHOR

John Humble grew up in an Evangelical Pentecostal church in the Deep South part of the United States. He was surrounded by love and good solid Bible teachings by his pastor, Sunday school teachers, and even a loving family that had Bible study and family prayer every evening.

The beginning of John's dilemma is that his parents were almost too good at following the desired pattern, and they exemplified to John what the unconditional love of God really looked like. As John began to ponder the unfathomable meaning of this love, he began to wonder why certain scriptures in the Bible tell stories about a harsh Being that does not match the description of the love that he was shown by his family and local church growing up. As John began to read and study the scriptures more and more, it only seemed to increase the number of questions that he had.

Today, John teaches an adult Sunday school class in Tulsa, Oklahoma, as a lay person who has never had any formal collegiate Bible training, but who has studied the words, the culture, the history, and the nuances of meaning in this book called the Bible all his life. He still has questions, and he is still studying....